Get Up, Sam!

by Cameron Macintosh

illustrated by Dan Widdowson

OXFORD
UNIVERSITY PRESS

2

Sam is sick.
Sam is sad.

Mum got the duck.

Dad got the rocket.

Sam did not pick it up.

Mum ran to pull on the sock.

Sam did not pick it up.

I miss Tess!

Dad ran to get Tess.

Tess!

Sam got up to pat Tess.

Sam is not sad!